I0203404

Corporations Are People, Too!

Other Books by Jerome Sala

Spaz Attack (STARE Press, 1980)
I Am Not a Juvenile Delinquent (STARE Press, 1985)
The Trip (The Highlander Press, 1987)
Raw Deal: New and Selected Poems, 1980-94 (Jensen/Daniels, 1994)
Look Slimmer Instantly (Soft Skull Press, 2005)
The Cheapskates (Lunar Chandelier Press, 2014)

Corporations Are People, Too!

Poems by

Jerome Sala

NQ Books™

The New York Quarterly Foundation, Inc.
New York, New York

NYQ Books™ is an imprint of The New York Quarterly Foundation, Inc.

The New York Quarterly Foundation, Inc.
P. O. Box 2015
Old Chelsea Station
New York, NY 10113

www.nyq.org

Copyright © 2017 by Jerome Sala

All rights reserved. No part of this book may be used or reproduced in any manner whatsoever without written permission of the author except in the case of brief quotations embodied in critical articles and reviews. This is a work of literature. Names, characters, businesses, places, events and incidents are either the products of the author's imagination or used in a fictitious manner. Any resemblance to actual persons, living or dead, or actual events is purely coincidental.

First Edition

Set in New Baskerville

Layout and Design by Raymond P. Hammond

Cover illustration: Roger Brown, American (1941- 1997), *Ferdinand and Imelda City*, 1986, oil on canvas, 72 x 48 in. © The School of the Art Institute of Chicago and the Brown family.

Author Photograph by Elaine Equi

Library of Congress Control Number: 2017930516

ISBN: 978-1-63045-043-4

for Elaine Equi

Contents

Work!

Corporate Sonnets

Consume!

Corporations Are People, Too!

To "Content"

you are like a word-picture-video flow
whose every element is special, but as part of a feed
(feeding whom?)
           also generic

a textual form of meat product:
like the old Aristotelian notion of "substance"
nothing in itself
but the something out of which all is made

like the Buddhist notion of emptiness
a zero
pregnant
with the psychedelic possibilities
of the 10,000 things
not to mention
the 84,000 forms of illumination
(but whose Samsaric version
most often manifests
as a googol's worth of banalities)

like Marx's "value"
made labor
between a bricklayer
a dog walker
a shoeshine boy
and an atomic scientist
equivalent
if translated into proportionate measure
of time, effort and general difficulty
or ease
so you
like Marx's dad
Hegel
turn quality
into quantity

helping to accomplish
in your case
not the discovery of the "Absolute"
but the absolutely
complete
commodification
of all
human
and
artificial
minds!

great spew
waterfall
that talks
blinks
sings
weeps
reaps
gain
from its own errors and ours
from our massive stupidity
and occasional brilliance

you dance with a life of your own
like coffee does
over the world market
doing our living for us
so we can dip into your
energizing stream
when exhausted
or check in with you
for a little daily enervation
when we are too hyped up to function
in the requisite depressed robotic
or positively positive-mental attitude fashion

then go back to work
or forced leisure
making voids
in the void
for angry
or ecstatic
voidoids
to fill the voids
of their oblong coffin
or birth channel
voids
and ours

with more content!

Work!

CORPORATE SONNETS

"There is a peculiar idiom that first emerged in such circles, full of bright, empty terms like vision, quality, stakeholder, leadership, excellence, innovation, strategic goals, or best practices. (Much of it traces back to 'self-actualization' movements...which were extremely popular in corporate boardrooms in the seventies, but it quickly became a language unto itself.)"

—David Graeber

"Two clichés make us laugh. A hundred clichés move us. For we sense dimly that the clichés are talking *among themselves*, and celebrating a reunion."

—Umberto Eco

1.

"What is a corporation?
What does it do?
To whom is it responsible?"
Does it care about you?

Is it buildings, companies,
Documents, waste?
Is it a subject, object, aggregate,
A function, a movement, a place?

Is it an agent we create
To explain what we do?
Is it shorthand for a process
That does things to you?

Does it generate wealth?
Is it good for your health?

2.

I don't know if I still have the bandwidth
to think outside of the box. I'm good at
identifying the low-hanging fruit
but innovation? Disruptive technologies?
That stuff may be for the millennials
to decide. Good luck to them. As for me,
well, there comes a time in all our lives
when you've got to just drink the Kool-Aid
and get with the program. Ok, sure,
you've no longer got the mojo
to break down any silos, but at least your
morale is no longer in the toilet.
I'm still entrepreneurial and proactive,
I'm collaborative, competitively-priced and non-reactive.

3.

I'm a go-to resource for some
really cool native advertising.
This shit is like advertorials
on steroids: it's sponsored content, but
it offers real information for your
prospects. And compared to old-fashioned
banner ads, you can expect click-through
rates that go through the roof. Of course, there's
always the potential for abuse—
a reader could feel misdirected,
confused, betrayed, if you look or sound
too close to your host site, but there's no
need whatsoever to take it that far:
give them something good, and your *brand* will be the star.

4.

There is the real responsive and the
fake responsive, he said, but none of
us knew how to respond to his response
to the questioner who asked, non-
innocently enough, about the
empirical, was it still valid,
or was advertising now purely
about vision, intuition, theory—
the non-narrative, polyvalent
nature of the Real? The real response,
I suddenly intuited him to be
thinking, wasn't about the ad, but us:
"It's not whether they say yes, no or don't know:
it's about if we play hard to get, or give them a go."

5.

I'm here to give you some intel on a
robust new app. But first, I'd like you to
reach out to your team to assure them that
this doesn't mean they'll be downsized, or that
adapting this is part of a general
corporate restructuring. They should be
excited by the new functionality
this product will offer, and the chance it
gives them to upgrade their skills. This program
is fast becoming a key component of
industry best practices, speeding the whole
decisioning process. "Hey people," I'd
say, "it is what it is, so here's my ask:
give it a chance to streamline your daily tasks."

6.

He said we could avoid brandpocalypse
by practicing data stewardship.
But have you ever met a brand whose
life was rescued by a deep data dive?
Perhaps what he meant to say was that
data mining plus repositioning
can save your brand, your product, your ass
(data freaks tend to speak in extremes
to close a deal)—but this should also
light up your bullshit detectors.
It's not like it's really a science,
despite the algorithms they brandish.
Shit, I doubt if data can even tell you why
your brand actually met its demise.

7.

As your manager, I've got a couple
of asks for you. It's not that I don't
admire your passion for the work—
this is your profession, after all—
but you've got to learn to separate
the facts from the emotions more.
Remember, *we're* the grown-ups; *they're*
the kids. That's what they pay us for. I've
got you rated as an above-average
performer, but in my book, you could
be a real star—someone who indexes
a full forty-five percent above
the baseline—which equals a hefty chunk of change.
So if I push you, don't look at me strange.

8.

Brands drive customers, but to where?
To all the engagement a product can bear?
Is "brand" another name for a dream?
The idea you can sell and still mean
Something to that well-defined someone
You know only in the abstract, but have fun
Thinking about, as if they were a friend:
The receiver of a message sent?
One created by the precise calculation
Of the demo and psychographic imagination?
A being born from the consumer research lab,
A faceless particular on which you keep tabs?
A bundle of buying habits charted on a graph,
Refigured formulaically through algorithmic math?

9.

— *After Ted Berrigan,* Sonnets, *37*

It is light. I am awake. And horrible fears
form a fist in my chest. Steve Jobs is dead.
The wild gray night surrenders to the boldly iterative day.
I worry that I need vastly better analytic tools
to monetize my idiosyncrasies
and enhance my progress toward career optimization.
My career is my poem. It is light. I
am awake. I need vastly better analytic tools
to optimize my career. I pin my favorite motivational quotes
to the cubicle wall. I school myself with vast
analytic tools. It is light. Motivational quotes
punctuate the boldly iterative day. I
am awake. A horrible fear forms a fist
in my career, in my poem, in the thought "Steve Jobs is dead."

10.

I'm wearing a lot of hats lately
and it really makes me step outside
of my comfort zone. But I've always
believed that you're in the wrong job
if you don't feel incompetent
at least 50% of the time.
My personal *ah-ha* moment
came one morning, when I had a tough
love talk with myself in the mirror.
Self, I said to myself, after looking
at myself long and hard, *are you
on the side of the bureaucrats
or the entrepreneurs?* That's when I took
responsibility: I burned all the rule books.

11.

—*After Spenser,* Ruins of Rome, *3*

You search for the corporation in the corporation
O intern, hoping to secure your career.
But the body you would inhabit has vanished,
Its limbs scattered offshore and near.

A career now a mere superstition—
A precious fetish from another time:
Something like a sonnet in the tradition
Of rhyme, meter and fourteen lines.

Until this body reassemble,
Your job will be fluid, like identity.
For thanks to the fury of globalization,
It can't tell its mind from its private parts or extremities:

To be incorporated for a brief moment as staff
Is not so different from being part of the riff-raff.

12-13.

She came to work that day looking for
happiness. Little did she know what
we had planned for her. And someone should
have told her, anyway, that work isn't for that.
It's for other things. Not the obvious
ones like making a living, but strange things.
Think entering a swamp, the dragonflies
flitting nervously as their programming orders.
Then a sudden frog leaps and eats one,
wings peeking from its jaws, happy
its life (the frog's, that is) has nothing to do
with a haiku. But the dragonfly, well,
you can imagine right before its life ends,
it's dreaming, in terror, about ways to transcend.

The sublime mysteries of predation
are waiting for us, among other things,
as we ride the singing elevators
to our floor: that open workspace where you
stare orb to orb at your fellow aliens:
where one eats and is eaten with such frequency
it's hard to tell the eater from the food.
Where there's always something to transcend
because the end is always near. But here,
it's the system that rules that hungry
impulse, with a rude insistence that its rule
makes the rules, rules that seem natural,
and therefore, naturally, folly to avoid —
but since they're impossible to follow,
perhaps they're just a ploy?

14.

Those days when we triumphed through "post-traumatic growth"
And learned optimism like you would a foreign language:
The bad dreams still followed us, but we heard them as ghost
Conversations, the kind you could ignore or just leave dangling—

A phone ringing in a hurricane, no one asks you to answer.
It was the time of creepy quiet, of big rooms with empty cubes,
Of a silence so silent, you'd hire up freelancers
Just to make small talk, laugh big laughs and pretend to be moved.

In this era of the aftermath, when after-images glowed,
Photographs of the fallen in our minds still not poked
From the frames of our inner movies, how slowly
We got used to it—and its diet of apocalyptic jokes.

Then, through "shifting and persisting" a "growth mindset" returned:
Of course, with the knowledge you might be the next to get burned.

15.

It was about that time when I started thinking of the great escape,
And people joked about Papillion—and being the last on the island.
I managed a few messages to the outside, feelers transmitted privately
Via the careerist underground. They told me what it would take

To make a break. I assembled what I could, from the little to which
   I had access—mostly fakes
I paid dearly for in, uh, "favors," if you know what I mean.
Anyway, it was the usual stuff: guns carved from soap, painted
With shoe black, Spiderman-like twine that you could swing

Over or between buildings in the hopes of someday
Descending gracefully into the crowded street below.
"If anyone asks, tell them I went for a walk around the block,"
I imagined myself saying, when great moment arrived.

What I actually did, when my mind entered this mode,
Was more secret and banal—that's why the above is all in code.

16.

Did you know that 65% of adults will be using
Internet-connected devices and/or watching TV
While they read your poems? Even if you don't write
Or read poetry—and less than 6% of U.S. citizens do nowadays—
Such findings should send up a red flag, as they suggest
That we all need to optimize our communications—
Even those as simple as our grunts during copulation or
For that matter, defecation (seeing as only 7% of our messages
Are conveyed through words, anyway). How then, can we get
Across what we need to say, in this new world of ours,
Crowded with so many competing voices, images and other
variously formatted types of messaging? Will you be among
The estimated 45% of Americans who finds a way to break through
  the clutter?
Or will you be with the others—the non-communicative motherfuckers?

17-18.

the corporation
e x p l o d e s
shatte rin g g g g g into a
n e t w o r k
like the moon at the beginning
of *Seveneves* by Neil Stephenson—
asteroids revolving around an absent center:
"That point—formerly the center of the moon, but now an
abstraction in space—
continued to revolve around the Earth
as it had done for billions of years"
so too the current hope for corporate survival
now a benzene ring of fragmentary freelance cells
sold as the "creative" answer to the old bureaucratic, organizational hell

the "hell" of the old "Fordist," "Taylorist" economy, that is
with its white collar Organization Men (sic), its rigid 9-5
its so-called manufacturing, blue-color, workers' aristocratic
P A R A D I S E
now DEFUNCT & DEBUNKED
by a breathtaking new order
and a new productive class, one that demands more
AUTONOMY! EMPOWERMENT! INNOVATION!
the mighty technocratic cognitariat
whose precarious march through evolving, revolving careers
is mobile, synaptic, rhizomatic
like the very brain itself!
and therefore "inevitable," a "natural order"
(one that doesn't, of course, respect any national border)

19.

I remember people saying "doi!"
I remember its variation: "duh!"
I remember "it is what it is" (when downsizing comes)
I remember "hump day"
I remember how new CEOs were "change agents"
I remember "how about a nice cup of shut the fuck up?"
I remember getting "energized" and "excited"
I remember bosses who said they were "tough but fair"
I remember how you had to "cut through the clutter"
I remember bull dogs, bulls in the china shop, and bull shitters
I remember spending time on "email maintenance"
I remember "didja' have a nice weekend?"
I remember "do ya' think?"
I remember "I'm sorry I have to tell you…this stinks, this really, really stinks…"

20.

A poem is like an ad: it's not what it says, but who says it.
What's taken for genius, the result not necessarily of wit
But of the sorts of cultural capital displayed along with it.
Writers sell shares in themselves on the literary stock exchange.
Some advance through connections, the famous names
They can drop or pick up. Great is their social acumen:
There are many in the genius class they are proud to call friends.
Others exhibit vast learning, plus an insider's view of trends.
They have an abnormal prescience about what's next to get hot,
Who the algorithmic spiders will search for, who will be forgot.
There's always the chance, I guess, someone drops in from nowhere,
An event so utopic, so mysterious, no wonder it's rare!
Some ascribe this to good karma, some say it's just mean—
The way certain poets seem *naturally* endowed with literary genes.

21.

When you develop your personal brand,
There are certain things you need to avoid.
Don't appear sullen. Pretend you're a fan
Of what brings your audience joy.

The audience you imagine, that is.
Be authentic with that phantom.
Don't be cloying. Fat is
The chance you'll attract them

If they know you're broke and in hot
Pursuit of a sale. Better to make a pitch
That's somewhat ironic: acknowledge that
We're all forced to sell, that it's unhip

To pretend otherwise:
Make them feel wise.

22.

(To the Mundane)

we try to hide
from you by going "off the grid"
or perhaps reply
to you as Sean Connery on a postcard
to Steve Jobs once did:

"For the final time NO
I don't want to be
in one of your fucking commercials!
You sir, are a mere computer salesman
and I am GODDAMNED James Bond!"

but the problem is, Sean Connery
never wrote that, nor got that irate:
it was a spoof devised
by some website as click bait.

23.

Staring at the cool, gray Formica
of a cubicle desktop, almost
the color of scissors: it's good
to return to a world where the wind
from the air conditioner massages
the mind, and emails thank you for
completing what you are fated
to do—as if the commanders
of each task feel like apologies
are in order for adding to your
annoyance: it's *their* annoyance
too, they want to tell you, and so on
up the chain: it's the way things run,
as politely as possible, under the gun.

24.

Unpeeled banana on desk, lying
on the small white square of a personalized
notepad: unappealing still life, even
when you add a bottle of sparkling lemon
Poland Spring water. The philosophers
say we humans are beings to whom sights,
sounds, and objects are never only that,
but lead somewhere—predicting futures.
This scene, though, and the computer screen
under which it rests, stays frozen—
a visual tautology, a sort
of mind statelessness: a frozen world
usually thought impossible to achieve.
Perhaps its stasis urges us to disbelieve.

25.

Because you're so passionate about
what you do, I advise you to keep
pushing the envelope, in order to
take your project to the next level.
Think of it as your first step on
the way to becoming a genuine
thought leader, someone who does
more than merely follow orders,
the kind of person who truly shakes up
the status quo. What better way to
prove your absolute indispensability
than by inventing one job after
another, and not only for you,
but for everyone in your crew?

26.

I want to get you that title you've been asking for,
But to do that, I need you to do something for me.
It's something that will challenge you a little more
Than before. Even better, it will add value to your team.

He said this and felt his head was a head in a cartoon.
A two dimensional hand descended into the spot
Where he lived for these few seconds, a tenant, roomed
In a mysterious square composed of Ben-Day dots,

And pried his head open, as if it were a can,
Wishing, it seemed, to fill it with some strange ingredient—
A gray ooze, featureless, formless, abstract, bland,
Replacing his brain and its ideas with a generic expedient:

And the ooze said: "What's so bad about corporate clichés—
They're just another tool to get you through the day."

27.

And then the ooze went on, readily supplying its ready-mades:
The need to "stay ahead of the pack," to "take responsibility,"
About how "if you're prepared, you don't need to be afraid."
Or if you are, how you should "act as if," and to the "best of your ability."

How if you give "your people" a "common platform
On which to communicate," and "stay aware of their needs,"
Then their jobs will no longer be mere jobs, but become a "program
For enrichment," through which they will continually "exceed

The customer's expectations." And, they will have true "career
Paths" they were called to follow, with tasks only they could do.
And on that path, they will just be asked to be themselves—if weird
So be it: business demands the authentic, management gurus

Assure us. This leads to psychic "wellness" and enhances trust:
People who work because they love it, not just because they must.

28.

The years I worked in corporate life, the air
Within the labyrinth was underscored
With a low buzz. Perhaps this was the AC
Or heat, depending on the season. Or maybe

The whisper of lights, computers, or the many tiny
Machines that ran all day and night: the breathing
Of technology. But now that I'm "packaged out,"
At home, sitting at my table, the freelance starting

To roll in, you'd think that sound would be gone.
But windows open or closed, it's here with me, still.
I hear its neutral moan in back of car horns, bus growl,
The squeal of drills in the building as it's repaired:

I heard it when I was young, on the way to the factory:
Like morning anxiety, it's something that follows me.

29.

And its uninflected language sends a message,
But only one: it says, simply, that things don't change,
That there was only ever now. But I wonder who's
Speaking? And despite such limited range,

With such relentless insistence? They say the system
That keeps things running, the concrete moments that
Flicker off and on in its abstract night, even the rhythm
Which our lives populate with their illustrious facts,

Is mindless, working for no purpose, but purposively
Churning out products, profits, even people and sentience—
An infinite brain with opaquely intricate circuitry
That prompts our smaller minds to finish its sentences:

And it's a great hobby, this interpretation of dreams,
As long as you resist what it all seems to mean.

30.

Corporations are people, too!
It's true.
They worry about death, taxes, healthcare, outsourcing, all that stuff,
And sometimes they've got it tough,

Just like you. Corporations are people too!
Monsanto, IBM, Microsoft, Nike and PepsiCo,
Are no different from Eunice, Harvey, or Mary Jo.
It's just that one tries to "make money," while the other "accrues,"

'Cause corporations are people, too!
One looks like a big old building stuck in the street;
The other pounds the pavement with tiny feet.
One can break an economy, but the other can get pretty damn rude:

And now both talk like hipsters, just to seem cool.
'Cause corporations are people, too!

Consume!

This One's for You

Once someone heard the old Broadway song that went
"I've got to be me, who else can I be?"
And they *were* that me.

And the more they were that me
The more they saw that me.

The street signs
The ads that popped up on the computer
After a while even the TV shows
The movies
The tunes
All agreed:

"You've got to be that me you're thinking of
Who else can you be?"

And each and every one of them added:

"But you need help
In order to be the real me
In order to speak and sing from the real me's soul

And that's why we're here.
We've come into your life to help you be you.
That's what matters most to us—
Because that's what matters most to you!"

Disposable Shavers of the World, Unite!

The disgusting way
we treat
the objects
that serve us,

relegating them
to the Hades world
of garbage
after we've had our way
with them.

They may be plastic or metal.
They may be made of tin
& the sins
of the colonial factories.

They may even refuse
to stare back at us
in accusation—

preferring rather
to speak amongst themselves
in a language
impenetrable
to the ears
of their exploiters.

But beware:

On the other side of the wall
of mass production
over the hedge
and through the woods
of even the most personalized manufacture—

even among

the mighty 3-D copiers
who promise to churn out
one-of-a-kind models
at turnaround speeds
of which we as yet cannot conceive—
another mode of being lurks.
One that whispers to itself
behind the generic buzz of street noise,
one that has its own plans for you.

Not just the specific you
but the abstract one—
the one left behind in blankness
when all its objects go away.

The Song of Gatorade

Your name sounds like a charity
For that very vicious variety
Of creatures who like to eat us
That's the way they greet us
A reptilian version of the frat haze
Down in the Florida Everglades.

Crazy jock joy juice
That sets our inner gators loose
From civilization's Park Rangers
Who've made the sports id an endangered
Species. Better than steroids, too:
You know that shit is bad for you!

When the coach wins the big one, you flow
Over his head: he gets a bath in your day-glow
And has to laugh it off. Though he looks pissed,
It's a ritual he wouldn't miss—
For the dry-headed coach takes the blame
For his team having choked during the big game.

In the movie *Idiocracy* they called you Brawndo,
And sprinkled you on crops to make them grow.
You burned them up instead.
Those idiot farmers had rocks in their heads,
To believe the Brawndo ads were right
When they preached the power of electrolytes.

Your sales are 3.3 billion dollars strong,
And you've been around so long
You're the leader, with a 50% market share—
No one else is even near!
But before you think you've got it made
Better watch out—here comes Powerade.

Pep

I drink from the cup
of Diet Dr. Pepper on ice—
so rich in its bouquet of 52 flavors
I think I can detect a bit of pepper in it,
along with a dash of cherry and a cola base,
the pepper catching on the tongue
of the mind, so I say to myself
pepper pepper pepper pepper pepper
speaking frankly among my personality fragments,
boldly in my crudeness.
Proud of this tone, its trivial pursuit of the trivial,
I descend into the maelstrom.

Ice Breakers Spearmint Mints

The natural joined with the artificial
to flavor this aid to social ease,
peppered with mint crystals
in the form of green pin pricks
embedded within a blank tablet.
False ice sooths as it melts, alluding
to the distant fires of sensual feeling
in that Eden some dream about,
before such tingles got framed in the prefabricated
commotion a promising commodity brings
to the market. Ice Breakers is owned
by the Hershey Company, today trading
at $90.23 a share on the NYSE. By the time
this poem touches home in the book of the future,
this figure will date it, throwing its status as a member
of the tribe that eschews contingency into doubt.
For now, though, in the dissolving present,
isn't it enough to simply feel cool?

Poland Spring Mandarin Orange

a slight accent
modulates your banality

it's enough to encourage me
to continue on
with the Poland Spring Experience:

you are an ideal:
in Plato's world
there must be room

for a form
that hugs to the norm
but with a smirk

that the smirk is orange
in your case
is merely incidental:

the small thrill you provide—
what carbonates our flighty world—
is the idea that normalcy
can be somewhat funky

it's a message
that hides inside many brands,
the secret to their animation—

what makes the surface
of our artificial world glow

the way neon sculpture once did
before we became bored with it
and the blank walls it hid

Planter's Planet

that commercial where the peanut
in the blue top hat, tapping his cane,
speaks like a politician from a yellow stage,
telling what look like uniformed but smiling
jocks in the audience that his nutritional energy
works hard for them and for us all:

nods of assent with that
"it makes sense" look—
assure us that the commodity
really is doing its job:

it tells us how smart we are
especially when we laugh
at its pitch so as to create
a friendly feeling between us

        who'd want to consume
        the cold equation
        that it is
        beneath the comedic mask
        of its bright
        cartoon personality?

        unless you were one of the few
        training to bend
        the time and space
        that keep us locked
        in the box of our minds

instead of all that hassle
the peanut presents a dream
to keep us grounded:

from the vantage of its neon world
we look back longingly to earth
it's how we convince ourselves
it's still there

we almost want to call it home

Kit Kat

*Give me a break, give me a break
Break me off a piece of that Kit Kat Bar

—*Advertising Jingle*

you are to be praised
for sticking to your guns:
still using an old-school jingle
to score your sweet propaganda

rather than just another "edgy," "bright," "fresh,"
and even more idiotic pop song
increasing its banality exponentially
through advertising's bad infinity of repetition

your sales pitch wears
the warm blanket
of community
of sharing
of friendship
of a benevolent social world

that exists for your 15 second commercial:

break me off a piece
of that Kit Kat bar

the world's competitive frenzy
melts
chocolate in a warm mouth

a wafer surprise inside
like an unexpected grace
a moment's mercy
a consolation prize for the loss of another day

no wonder it's the bar of choice
you receive
after the dehydrated bodily exhaustion
of a colonoscopy

58

Halls "Intense Cool" Cough Drops

On the aqua-green glass table
a shiny black bag
of *Halls Menthol-lyptus Cough Drops*—

"INTENSE COOL"

a state
any being
dressed in patent-leather-like plastic
can claim.

Back in the days of *punk*
there was a moment when
a thin brown vinyl zippered jacket
became more intensely cool
than any mere
black leather gear.

It was that flaunting of artifice
especially when worn
over a naked chest
hustler style
that made it so.

To embrace the cool of simulation
as a way of being real:
that was how the era rolled.

It was only by freezing out
the old fetish
with one even more icy
that the skin
could begin
to feel again.

It's a little like the way
these cough drops work:

their menthol so chilly
they open blocked passageways—

suddenly you can
not only breathe
but your taste returns
bringing with it a hunger
for strange new flavors.

Blistex Blues

Two small, dark-blue jars of Blistex lip balm stare like eyes.
Are they kind, neutral, or reproachful? It's hard to tell.
Does this ring a bell?
Reason says objects don't emote, but it lies.

I know, I know, they're just mass-produced.
And it's said they don't possess an aura.
They're more like metallic, robotic (at best!) flora,
Part of a conspiracy to keep us in a system-induced

Coma—so we miss everything more substantial,
I.e., an inner life, a hidden talent, a secret task
Grander than this moment—something meant to last
Longer than dry lips, something that unlocks our potential.

But that's a lot of guilt to hang on a jar of balm,
Especially if it's simply designed to sell,
To relieve a discomfort that's small.
Is it really a sin to pursue a little calm?

Beaming

The subject line on the email reads
       "Good Day Sunshine!"
It's an ad for jewelry
whose tagline is:

    "Designed for the Journey."

Inside it says:

    "Radiant. Happy.
    & Absolutely Striking.

But enough about you!"

    followed by a picture of a
    "Sunbeam Necklace"

which looks like the stylized edge of a sun
 at half-moon—
    a golden curve

      into which

  you can slip your neck.

  Is the sun still a god?

I think of Neil Gaiman's novel *American Gods*

       in which
the old gods want back in

    but they've been pushed aside

by the shiny new gods of popular culture

    who live in the new Olympus
of Hollywood

or NYC penthouses

the old gods consigned to shanty towns

deep in the pores
of irrelevancy

and they're irritated, ill

they need belief to live

like a vampire needs blood

and they starve
until the underground realizes
they still provide favors—

but at a terrible cost!

The Sunbeam Necklace
is $249.00

is framed at the edges
by citrine, a stone
the ad says, that brings you

"radiance
happiness
awareness"

the necklace thus
"worthy of any goddess"
even though it's only
gold plated
over gun metal
and brass

One Issue Left

The magazine had a rage for orders
And desperately wanted yours.
It feels good to be desired.
It knew this and told you so,

In the letters and emails it sent:
You are the type of reader
We want with us. Not everyone
Understands what we do,

But you do. Why not join others
Who know what you know? And then,
Together, we can change something.
We'll figure out exactly what that is

When the time is right. We have a process,
And we know that it works. Won't you
Jump into its mighty flow? Won't you
Work it with us? Let us know. But soon.

Please. Your subscription's about to run out.

Gift Card

Comes in an official gray envelope.
The subdued, yet rich, blue type reads:

Rewards Information Enclosed

I have earned these points
through the good behavior
of my many purchases
via the original card provided me
with the good wishes
of the corporation it proudly represents.

And as I rip the envelope open
it is with the particularly abstract joy
one experiences
by stepping into the self-reflexive loop
of money that makes money
a card that gives birth to another card.

As my reward
with this card
I can buy the science fiction novel
where robots enslaved to corporations
who war with each other on behalf of them
in a nearly apocalyptic
"battle of the brands"
decide to turn on their masters
machines raging against the giant machine.

Who do you think wins?

I make my purchase now
from one of the largest corporations
in universal history
with branches, it is rumored
among the earthlike planets
of the Alpha Centauri system itself.

And if the robots win, I wonder
will the theoretically more egalitarian
robot world they achieve
and the new robot network they install
be better or worse
than the rigid, hierarchical
robot world they have overcome?

My book is downloading now.

Maggie

Powerful gloom that emanates from that film:
Young people bit by zombies, slowly start to change.
Their parents are stumped as to what to do.
But once their fellow humans start to smell like meat,
A point of no return has been reached. It's either
Quarantine—a place where folks of all states
In their transformation are locked together,
Allowed to simply devour each other—or they're given
A potion that kills them slowly, painfully, extremely so.
The easiest answer for all involved is the hardest:
A parent must blow the child's head off with a gun.
But who can do this when the kid's not undead yet?
Lucky for dad, his daughter jumps off the roof.

The Question

How low
how low
how low
will
it
go?

The price of sweet, sweet, sweet crude.

That's the question all the markets are asking.

And it's my question too, if I may be so rude
as to suggest
and I don't mean this in jest
that many of our most profound, internal moods
depend
in ways we do not yet fully comprehend
on the rise and fall of the objective price of crude!

Sweet crude
meaning less than 0.5% sulfur content
meaning unlike the icy heavy water from a comet
it does not smell like rotten eggs
meaning it earns a $15 a barrel premium over the sour stuff

How low?

For wind power doth blow in oil's face
and sun power doth beat upon its back
and shale rock doth crack!
as the mighty horizontal drills frack
shaking up the very terran unconscious

so that the earth
we walk upon
shatters beneath
like ice in a glass

spiking the underground
with hydro carbons
resulting in cheaper oil to drive our cars on
and drinking water that catches fire!

How low?

It is written that when Gertrude Stein died
she asked Alice B. Toklas, "What, Alice, is the answer?"
and when she got no reply
she sighed
and simply said:
 "very well, then, what is the question?"

Today we still don't know the answer
but at least the question is clear:

How low will the price of crude go?

The sweet, sweet crude whose price per barrel
is bent
out of shape, by the Brent
benchmark!

And no other.
We will accept no substitutes in our global market!

Since summer
the price has dropped 45%
with no bottom in sight!

And so now, the Chinese can demand a cut rate deal from the
  Nigerians!
And so now, Putin can claim the drop is a conspiracy to destroy
  Mother Russia!
And so now, the Saudis refuse to cut back on production in order
  to lowball the Texas shale wildcats.

How low?

And when the sun burns bright enough
and the wind blows hard enough
so that even the price of shale
begins to pale
and the oil economy is finally cast out from the earth's temple...
will this mean that for the last 150 years or so
all the glories of our modernism and postmodernism
all the wonderful avant-gardes and boring mainstreams
all the smart and dumb technologies
all the revolutionary and reactionary political theories
all our religious revivals and denials
have been marred by a consciousness that is simply crude?

In other words
that all our great creations are something like those of Jethro
in the *Beverly Hillbillies* TV series of old
who, once intoxicated by Texas Tea
and the great profits it brought his family
decided to become a Beatnik artist
and began sculpting shapeless abstract works from chewing gum!

And without oil, who will fund the fundamentalists?

How low will it go?

Speculate!

Feudalism

gave way to
Capitalism
which continued the feud

with a different set of kings
and a different brand
of serfs

Top Down Management

Soon NFL Sunday begins
But isn't it time to start that *personal* highlight reel
You've been thinking about—the one that captures
All those things you've walked away from
Just in time, and are glad of it? Those potentialities are still
Out there, living their own lives, in the negative dimension opened up
By your last minute retreat, and though they don't miss you
They are grateful, and are forever so, for the engine of your fantasy.
Ghost beings of the cerebral irresolute—
Like the smile on a pumpkin, a giraffe, or an antique graph,
They are and are not there at the same time, much as the famous cat
Who is and is not dead or alive in Schrodinger's box,
Or like Ant-Man, the Wasp, or the Incredible Shrinking Man
Once they've entered a quantum realm.
But what really, definitively, *is* here or not these days—
The mind floating like a chaotic weather system
Over the stodgy, conservative (if frilly) ruffles of the brain—
As if it's bent on proving to itself that what would determine it
Doesn't call all the shots. Like the stock market,
It wants to prove that speculation is more than an airy nothingness,
And it needs no poet to bring it down to the earth
Whose rotation it now controls.
It's as if some gremlin has snuck behind the Big Board
And turned the calculation tables upside down:
Now the abstract figures are more real
Than the all the reals they would abbreviate.

Don't Make Any Plans

The strategic planner thought that his talent
for dazzling strategic plans
was proof that his destiny
was to join the canon—
that he was in fact part of the grand lineage of
some of the most important strategic planners
in the history of strategic planning—
but now
not only his own fate
but the history of strategic planning
as strategic planners
have heretofore envisioned it
was in jeopardy
for
compared
to the daring
advances in statistical selection and quantification
leading to new techniques which allow for the first time
a total annihilation of the human "decisioning" process
the algorithmic brain-like waves generated by the hyper-math
of the hub's new quantum processors
could now do the work
of a thousand strategic planners
with the "don't-even-need-to-think-about-it" confidence
that arises when artificial intelligence begins to operate
with the natural efficiency
of the human brain's input processing modules.
And yet ethnographic research
conducted among the dwindling subculture of human SPs
reveals an almost religious devotion
to the values of human error:
"we learn better, more quickly, more creatively
than our replacements"
claim the soon-to-be-out-of-work.
"These mistakes push our evolution forward
naturally selecting sheep over goats
or

if the economy calls for it
goats, or even ghosts, over sheep
or for that matter
spreadsheets.
And while it's true that due
to daily, bureaucratic busy-work
best left to machines
we are often spread too thin
and that our strategies themselves suffer as a result
of the time starvation of daily corporate life
it would be a shame to throw out the bodies of us planners
via the bath water
of the simulacrum of our brains.
This merely reinstitutes the mind/body contradiction
that brought down the house of Modernism
whose own planners seemed unaware of the maxim
'no body/no thought.'
The 'singularity' is a myth,
for the simulated mind depends
upon hands clacking away at keys."
It's enough to make you weak in the knees
this flight
from human strife
into its mirror world
where all its quirks are repressed
while all the meanwhile
angry tentacles grow Triffid-like
over the melting houses of computer servers
as the earth eats itself
thanks to the atmosphere's anthology of maladies.
At some point, the wilds will reclaim their real estate
from not only the human
but virtual mind
as if to remind
the no one who is listening
that the great "outside"
has never left.

The Tale of the Badass Dad

I laughed at the idea of generational politics,
before I was jumped by the 5,000-year-old dad.
Motherfucker kicked my ass bad—
got here from some time travel holodeck
after a fight with Oedipus and Tyrannosaurus Rex—
both were messaging his girl
in some shit hole of the ancient world.

He smacked me hard upside my head.
"Bitch, that was just to get your attention," he said.
And when I began to snivel, he knew that I was ready
to listen to his crap—some heady
bullshit that turned an old windbag like him red:
the old prick forgot to take his meds
(if they had them back there, from where he fled).

"When I tripped through this here vorpal porthole,
I wasn't lookin' for trouble,
but I saw you fuckups needed help—and on the double—
so I hauled ass into your space.
You jerkoffs have made a total disgrace
of your environs: I'm hearing sirens
everywhere—and is that from burning tires,
that stench like frying rubber? Or is that the future
I'm smelling—my sense of time got butchered."

But it wasn't just gloom and doom the old bastard preached,
but something harder to fathom. He reached
and out of his back pocket pulled some kind of scripture,
mysterious, incomprehensible words and pictures,
of maybe UFOs, but then again, maybe just cones, trapezoids,
parallelograms, a few cigars, guitars, ellipsoids,
a code, or script—or evidence of a schizoid
mind, philosophy, god or religion. His generation
apparently struggled mightily with articulation.

And then this ancient crank started blabbing something bad
about the opportunities we missed, how he was almost glad
we're about to lose our shit, the barbarian world we built—
its cyclopean monoliths, its savage executions, its axial tilt.
It's a joint where confusion cranks itself higher
than a Babylonian tower.
Then he pulled out an oil-slick comb:
"In my day, we used it as pomade, that black foam
You feed your robots with:
You and your toys—you're all full of shit."

"But most of us know this, Mr. Daddio," I swore,
"If you want my attention, you gotta' do more."
"Yeah, you all know a lotta' shit," he replied.
"But the way you all act, makes me think you lie.
It's like you're all wearing helmets, hoods or blindfolds,
so you can't see straight or read the signposts
that warn about the *Do Not Enter* zones.
Soon you'll be without life, limb or mobile phones."

Our conversation went on, stunted, irregular like that.
We kept throwing barbs; two assholes chewing the fat.
Nuclear winter, global warming, a viral menace:
this nihilist couldn't wait for a world without us in it.
"But I thought you came here to help—I don't see
how your bloodthirsty rant will help us cheat
the apocalypse breathing down our necks.
We've already got tribes here celebrating our wreck."

And then the old coot said, "I think I changed my mind.
So what if I'm unpredictable: I come from another time.
One that's gone, that wants the future gone, too:
it's no fun not being there, while there's still all of you
crawling around your big ass ant farm,
building your space stations, colonizing in swarms.
Your greatest poet is the one who wrote 'RAID KILLS BUGS DEAD!'"
And with that half-assed thought, back to Big Zero he fled.

78

Chicken Shit

And the notation written on the back of the chicken
in my dream
was a mysterious question mark
set equidistantly between two burly dice
by which I understood to mean
that one should not chicken out in the face
of the great randomness
but rather cast one's own dice
in bravery or cowardice
without so much as a squawk.

Great noble domesticated chicken
you, too, are a gamble.
Onward you go
a frazzled meatsicle on the edge of the causal void
an abstract painting
rendered with nervous strokes and splash
a riddle of white on a whiter canvas—

except the chicken experiences this subjectively
and in color
its dreams anticipate escape
from the butchers and pluckers of this world.
And sometimes, if rarely,
those dreams come true.

Oh, Well

Was it really so bad,
the age of arthouse cinema?

People felt going to the show
was like entering a museum,

while those who went to a museum
felt as if they were entering a church,

and those who entered churches
often did so because they wanted to view the art.

Mayakovsky entered the Revolution,
it is written, as one would enter his own home.

In the haunted house film,
there is always a room you are forbidden to enter—

the actors always enter it anyway—
they are compelled to,

to ignite the engine of the film.
The ghost inevitably is a disappointment—

like arthouse cinema was to the moviegoer,
like the holy museum was to those searching for rebellious art,

like the church was to the true believer,
like the revolution was to Mayakovsky.

Improving Your Brain Performance

Yes, there have been some exciting advances.
I'm a big advocate
of those emulsified protein crackers,
seasoned with Saturnalian seaweed.
It seems this mixture allows neurons to overthrow
their oppressive helix programmers
and leap forward across the synaptic plains,
leading aggressively luminous light brigades
through the wilderness of daily thought.
Headaches have been reported, unfortunately,
by some entities,
though these folks may be afflicted with defective vessels,
and thus their tendency is to fall back into entropic thought patterns
just because these make them feel more warm, fuzzy and nostalgic.
But we, in this post-nostalgic age, must ask
if there is really a place for them
in the political economy of the ingenious.
Why there are those among us
who can turn a bed and breakfast racket
into a symphony of intensified international service.
Others can dissolve the resistance of facts
in the acid of their entrepreneurial visions,
and then are those who dazzle
with their techno-biological shamanism,
concocting new breeds of attitude, designed
to conquer through their bracing shamelessness.
Someday these people, our people,
will be the only ones left.
Then we can start talking about
an equal distribution of competitive weapons,
level battlefields,
mutually assured electrified barbed wire fences,
and all the rest of that hearts and flowers shit.

Bones

In that museum,
great tusks
trumpet into sight.

They poke their space, hoping
to recall the age in which they dominated,
and when children's eyes meet them

they still compel attention—

their own wooly mastodon bodies,
once great trombones themselves,
now tortured out of existence.

The populations
through which they once cut a path
with their living thunder,

now thumb screwed
to the collapsing walls
of another demanding rule.

The bandits who first poached them
from the forbidden zones
now pure dust, like the plains they robbed.

But here the bare bones remain
insisting on a place:

pin points
tiny moons

reflected in the eyes
of the children
of their conquerors.

The War Against the War on Porn

When the tribe of mental filter manufacturers deserts its post,
guarding civilization from its disreputable disputations,
there's no telling what the consequent barbarian flood
will wash over the barriers.
I, for one,
demand a reinstitution of the split-screen personality.
That is my right
as a citizen who believes
that every sublimation requires a transparent underside,
where, for a price,
folks can gain admission to the aquarium of the National Dream.
There are strange, striped sharks in this tank,
some genetically sutured to prehistoric crocodiles.
During hiccups in the fantasy cycle,
when the tank bursts its sides,
they tend to be lifted out of their depth on filthy waves
or spun through the dirty air that smooches the dreamer's window
every time a midnight traffic jam lets out a secular belch
and the stars rattle in the sky, like teeth in the mad mouth
of someone who's just taken an awesome punch.

A Spy in the Bahamas

A big dog barks all morning,
just the kind of rooster
a friendly neo-imperialist like myself
would love to ignore. But, like the crimes
of the developed world, as they blossom
into the breathtaking varieties of blowback,
such sharp little explosions become increasingly
difficult to ignore, especially when you're suffering
from the emotional hangover
a failed assassination or coup can engender.
I feel a sort of invisibility that frightens me.
Each nonchalant smile, erupting from under
the cool brim of a Panama hat,
the tinkle of ice that seems to follow me around,
the occasional yawn of a bored plane overhead—
it's a landscape where I can feel
the eyes of the malevolently curious at my back.
Perhaps the more so because all seem so relaxed,
and with even a cool friendliness. Maybe
I should stop reading conventional manners
as if they were fables, broadcasting news
from the underworld. All I know is that
when I leave this beautiful isle I won't,
like Orpheus, make the mistake of looking back.
That is, of course, unless I hear the wind rustle
in just that way that is the wrong way.

Interstellar

Albert Camus crashed his car into a wall,
But the bricks paid him no mind.
They were too busy doing time,
Forming a boring grid, over which his legend could crawl.

A grid that mimed the word "blankness"
To the existentialist, whose philosophy, though now passé,
Once enjoyed a certain teenage-angst type heyday,
Loved, its lovers held, for its authentic frankness

About the void its writers and artists created—
The one they found at the center of the human soul,
Replaced today by the idea of sublime black holes,
Holes out there, not in here, seemingly unrelated

To the arty voids of years ago.
Sometimes I miss them, or their idea,
They gave a person something to be free of,
But now that history's over, we're all free (or so we're told).

And the voids, out there, in the universe,
Offer the chance to conquer scary time and space—
So that when the earth runs dry, we'll find another place.
If you can shoot through a black hole, on the reverse

Side (it's believed), you'll find planets ready for life.
Something like big green houses where you can plant
Your ass, and the asses of your children, and
Their children's children: until another galaxy is rife

With lots of such progeny, building walls, at first to protect,
Later to knock their heads into, as the cycle
Turns its wheels: the struggle for survival goes viral,
And all of human history resurrects.

The Agent

The tune cared for me.

It said: you belong to me,
as it implanted its rhythm within.

It was always on.

Maybe life would go on around it,
but there was no done,
no after,
under its powerful rain.

I didn't care about
what it told me I cared about,
but still,
it went on.

If you beg it to stop,
this is proof

of its victory.

Better Than You

"You wisest Grecians, pardon me this brag."
— *Shakespeare*

Isn't it strange that the gunk of the universe, that amorphous blob,
That gives rise to all things, makes each and every one of them snobs?
Not just the boring human kind, a version of snobbery we all know
(Where you think you think or feel more nobly than those below
Or above you on the great chain of classes), but the snobbery of all,
Alive or dead, on earth, in heaven, known, unknown, big or small,
Stupid or smart, serious or comic, violent or pacific. Outside my window
Are many examples: the shadow that bends flexibly akimbo
Feels it's cooler than the stiff, conventional one that's just straight.
The person who crosses with the light feels more together than one
   who's late.
Or take the simple tree that stretches its arms above the city's traffic—
It thinks it's more natural and naturally superior to the machines it
   laughs at.
And better than people, too, who seem more machine-like than organic,
Possessed by cars, cellphones—all the types of things Blake called Satanic,
In a moment of Romantic snobbery that produced a haughty poem.
To be is to brag, no matter the degree of reality you think you own.
The gene isn't really selfish, it's just a pile of chemicals with attitude,
And RNA thinks it's cooler than its sibling DNA, citing the platitude
That it started life, liberty and natural selection, before its mirror self
Arrived on the scene. Getting somewhere first usually creates a belief
That one is superior to what comes after. And to be actual
Is to feel more worthy than to be imagined: it's assumed that just to
   be factual
Endows one with a sort of sainthood. Snobbery allows the unrhymed line
To think it's better than its opposite, who it sees as old-fashioned and
   phony—
Feeling itself more authentic, closer to a "real voice" and all the baloney
That goes along with such appeals to the so-called heart. But I can tell,
O brilliant Reader, that you're too smart for all that crap about keeping
   it real.
And you know that I know of your sophistication, and since we both
   understand,
Snobs like us also know to leave this pompous poem, before it gets
   out of hand.

Speculations

Frank O'Hara

Looking at his book the other day, I thought it was like a type of party that is no longer thrown, to which, even if it were, you would never be invited. But how beautiful it still seems!

A Barbarian in Paris

On my first day in Paris, I discovered the French invented the East Village. Who knew?

It's Easy

Banality
is Reality.

At the Pompidou

Already in 1973, Gerhard Richter had figured it out. That rather than history, things were now all happening in an eternal present, but a highly regimented one. One resembling a somewhat colorful grid.

Mumbo-Jumbo

The voice of power is cryptic.

Funny How That Works

It turns out the Great Communicator was especially good at telling people to shut up.

Kim Stanley Robinson Was Right

If global warming turns New York City into Venice, after a few hundred years, the inhabitants will start rationalizing that it was a good thing—and that they're glad it happened.

Everyone Is an Expert About Something

An ad is never about the products, brands or offers it features—first and foremost, it is about other ads. Some ads, in fact, assume an almost encyclopedic knowledge of popular culture and the genres of advertising—and they are right to do so. No matter their social background, all consumers own PhDs in advertising.

I was wondering

...where to go with it all, when the all evaporated even more quickly than the where.

Related?

A "gag" can be a joke or a choke.

The Spectral

Stained glass butterfly
and raspy voice-over
of the arty horror film.
A valley of swans.
Sometimes that's enough.

Respect Your Reporting Faculties

The thing I like most about simulation
is its healthy respect for the Real.
An imitation is an imitation is an imitation,
an echo chamber of circumspection by which you feel

your way around in the world: imagination
being an extra sense, a limb, a mental metal detector
to assess your prospects in advance, by gradation
between what you sense and what there is, a reflector

that helps you move between the two without
jumping headfirst into a snow bank you don't know,
haven't tested for sharp objects. It also keeps your mouth
shut in a crowd of strangers: maybe they're foes—

members of a tribe that hates your sort
for some reason impossible to anticipate.
The mind needs to add logistical support
to cut its path through an ordinary day.

The Uninvited

Some wish, swept under the sweat of the day
by an anonymous broom—call it chance if you need
a name. I'm mostly OK in the world of namelessness,
a bit like the shadow realms of the Ancients—
rugged corridors of nothing but conventional responses—
the relentless rituals that keep you secluded from the otherwise mild
gray twilight of chaos. You can hear that regularity in the street
tuned to the motors of the busses, the slamming of car doors,
the ambient laughs, shrieks and blips of indistinguishable sentences
that keep the air busy with their confetti, as if to assure you
there are no bits of the universe lacking dusty particles
to announce, in advance, each corner. When you do
find one down which to turn, it almost feels like you're walking
through the aftermath of some party or parade
you're glad you didn't attend:
if you were invited, that sense of hiding out in the midst
would disappear. You might be discovered by some sense
of responsibility, perhaps taking the form of a smiling person,
who suggests the two of you should have lunch.

Today in Erehwon

drill in the street

creating a black hole—
on the other side

the UTOPIA STAR SYSTEM

with green, earth-like planets

where all is well:

the worker who works the drill
& knows this

and drills

to go there

is a Starfleet Communist

a Galactic Anarchist

a technocratic
dream body & mind

from another future –

the imagination

of the present

gives way

to the invasion force:

TEAMSTERS OF ALPHA CENTURI

your moment is our moment

it even happens to be NOW!

Monsters!

The story you tell
Falls down a well.
It blooms down there.
It even grows fur.

You should've left it below
Asleep with the bones.
But thanks to your big mouth
The horror is roused.

Now it's climbing back up
To fuck the town up.
You can see the TV crews
Fighting for scoops.

Those monsters that appear
At the edge of the weird
Are persons from your words
Who have lost their reserve.

They're shouting at us.
They tip over a bus.
They're screaming at the crew.
They want no part of the news.

They liked their little world.
It was so quiet down there.
Sure, they were freaky.
Sure, they were weird.

Why'd you have to go
And let us all know?
They were better where they were,
Not part of the world.

At least that's what they say
On this horrible day—
People running down the street,
Monsters needing to eat.

In the Valley of the Allegorical Animals

And that night in my dream
I entered the Valley of the Allegorical Animals.

Each roamed its emerald pastures
                              with that flair
that comes from expressing one's purpose
with one's very being!

The pig that stands for fullness
        for happiness
                    for the ecstatic complacency
                              of the bourgeoisie
and therefore
                for the antique, the arcane
for the bourgeoisie no longer exist.

The owl
        that flies into the windshield
                    of the futurist
for as we know
owls are only wise to the past—
and its haunting gasp
like a drowning giant
struggling toward the surface of time.

                "The dog—
                    you may call him Old Yeller,"
                    the dream voice said,
                "And it's ok, you can ask
                    your allegory to speak—
                    even if he is a dog."
                The dog says
                "I'm so horny!
                    Lead me to nearest
                    pornographer's casting couch—

94

I promise
I won't piss on the furniture
because of my excitement
or my disgusting, inbred tendency to territorialize
or to please!"

The crow
Señor Somber Solitude
guardian of a midnight opium stash.
The crow has always stood for one thing only:
the crushed velvet decadent Romanticism of the 19th century.
He wants to be more
but his shiny being—
even with his Goldfinger-esque addiction to precious metals—
won't allow him.
Unlike the wild indeterminacies afforded the leisure class,
the crow is someone who must work a for a living
and this, the only job for which he receives symbolic wages
limits his identity, his ambitions, his potential for self-expression.

And as I walked through the dream valley of the allegorical animals
I realized that one need not fear a meaningless existence,
but rather the opposite—
for all here meant too much!

The cow in whose moo you hear
the anger of
resentful, forgotten gods.

The squirrel:
the con artist of the beasts:
he coaxes friendly gifts from those around him
and then, a miser,
acts as the nervous guardian of his meager treasure.

The snake, who teaches us
how to smile wickedly

and thus gain
the magnetism of the elect.

The platypus:
she reassures her students
that the impossible is not only possible
but nearby!

And then there's the wombat, the rug rat, the cane toad—proud of its poison
glands, the ray-finned catfish, the giraffe who spies on the naughtiness of
of the tree-dwelling crowd, the brute, fascist rhino, a reactionary of the old
old school, the industrious but warlike tiger ant, the brown recluse spider,
famous for his necrotic kiss...

> Each animal meaning more than the rest—
> so that the valley contains so many animals
> and so much meaning,
> that exploring it is rather like
> struggling to walk through a bowl of Jello
> tinged with molasses.

One can hardly bear
to live this way,
nearly smothered by significance
so that one longs
after a short visit
for the liberating blankness of the awake world
where things are bought and sold
and meaning is assigned to them
crudely
carelessly
arbitrarily
and for non-mysterious ends.

Next on the Agenda

As the legend of the market grew less enthralling,
So did the exploits of those who'd have none of it.
We gazed at the crashing waves of numerals
And longed for the day of a great turnaround.

But the Great Nation rose instead to regal prominence,
Or rather the nations, the whole of idea of nations,
Descended from the realm of ideals to greet us,
Though their flying, swimming and marching armies
Had yet to appear in the land of the frightened.

We dreamed of savage rulers, who flayed their frenemies alive
In dungeons lined with rabid dog cages. We saw dragons
Flying overhead to protect the armada of the just:
And the good sent more of the good troops to keep us feeling good.

And when nations beamed brighter than the old commodities,
Everyone swore allegiance to several:
Dancers, singers, actors, fans—all created a sovereignty
Or joined one—there was a principality for every flavor,
And each promised protection and love, warmth and steel.

And all you were asked for was your devotion—
Your tiny chatter throughout the infinite networks.
Plus, for a few comparatively modest "donations,"
A customized mythology of your very own could be yours.

The Drive

The stars are motivated by their desire to tell us the age of the
universe.
The lake is motivated by its need to differentiate itself from
the ocean—
Hence, it shows less emotion, favoring placidity over roar.
If the revolution ever arrives, they say it will be motivated by
the demand for justice
And an end to gross inequality—not merely the acquisition
of more commodities,
Or at least not only that. Hunger for living human flesh is what
motivates
The zombie. The horde? Its will to conform. The *given* by a need
to be here
Before anyone or anything else. The *wanted* by their ability to
escape notice
In a crowd, or even from the trillion watchful eyes of the
contemporary
Surveillance State. The ignorant are motivated by their wish to
stay that way,
At times going to great effort to avoid knowledge. The Market is
driven by quite
Mysterious motives, often indecipherable to human minds—this is
why it is often
Compared to a mighty deity or a hysterical neurotic—depending
upon the diversification
Of one's own portfolio. The mirror has much to teach us—it is
motivated by a love for
Creating doubles; so doing, it expresses its authentic being-in-the-
word through
The practice of duplicity. The philosopher Hegel tells us that
politicos who flatter
The powerful are motivated by a noble end: to obtain the favors
their constituencies need

To survive. Hence, you could say they sacrifice their own
   self-respect and reputation for
The sake of others: they are flacks for their flocks. The flag is
   motivated by the pleasure
It derives from being tickled by the wind—this allows it to forget
   the great violence
That called it into existence, and continues to maintain its
   meaning. The philosopher
Schopenhauer believed that the entire universe was motivated
   by a blind will,
Incomprehensible as a whole, but hinted at in the pleasures
   and pains of one's body: this
Is why those management books that harangue middle-executives
   on the need to motivate
Themselves and their staffs are puzzling: for all are motivated,
   so much so that those
Who pretend otherwise are hiding something from you
   or themselves, and thus, the first
Question one should ask about the so-called *unmotivated* is their
   motive for engaging in
The Herculean task of disguising their mighty motivation from you.
   Lumberjacks are
Motivated by their love of lumberjack style: they are said to have
   a fetish for plaid.
The Deal is motivated by the wish to be called good—either by
   the buyer or seller, or,
In some cases both, as in the famous "win-win situation." Bosses by
   the wish to be
Obeyed. Chips to be played, or for variety, the fear of being down.
   Triggers, by
The fingers that fondle them. Darts, by bullseyes, or the challenge
   of keeping shirt collars
Straight. Motivation itself is motivated by its destiny: to implant

Itself in all beings, both concrete and abstract, real and imagined.
  And the poem?
It is motivated simply by the need to continue. Even when it dreams
  of ending, it does so
In hopes of somewhere, sometime, somehow, beginning again—
  with a new set of words,
Emotions, ideas and yes, motivations. This poem is dreaming
  that dream as it speaks—
And it continues to do so, even now, as it stops.

Acknowledgments

Thanks to the editors of these magazines, where some of these poems first appeared: *Journal of Poetics Research, Ladowich, Plume, Posit, Southampton Review, Travel Tainted.*

"In the Valley of the Allegorical Animals" appeared in *Plume Anthology of Poetry 5*, edited by Daniel Lawless (Madhat Press, 2017).

Note

The first three lines and many of the terms/ideas of Sonnet 1
have been borrowed from Marina Welker's *Enacting the Corporation*
(University of California Press: 2014).

About the Author

Jerome Sala's books of poetry include cult classics such as *Spaz Attack, I Am Not a Juvenile Delinquent, The Trip, Raw Deal, Look Slimmer Instantly, Prom Night* (a collaboration with artist Tamara Gonzales), and *The Cheapskates.* His poetry and criticism have appeared in *The Best American Poetry* series, *The Nation, Evergreen Review, Pleiades, Conjunctions, Rolling Stone, The Brooklyn Rail, Journal of Poetics Research* and many others. Before moving to New York in the 80s, Sala and his spouse, poet Elaine Equi, did numerous readings together, helping to create Chicago's lively performance poetry scene. He has worked for many corporations of all kinds as a professional copywriter and has a Ph.D. in American Studies from New York University.

The New York Quarterly Foundation, Inc.

New York, New York

Poetry
Magazine

Since 1969

the NEW YORK QUARTERLY

Edgy, fresh, groundbreaking, eclectic—voices from all walks of life.

Definitely NOT your mama's poetry magazine!

The *New York Quarterly* has been defining the term contemporary American poetry since its first craft interview with W. H. Auden.

Interviews • Essays • and of course, lots of poems.

www.nyquarterly.org

No contest! That's correct, NYQ Books are NO CONTEST to other small presses because we do not support ourselves through contests. Our books are carefully selected by invitation only, so you know that NYQ Books are produced with the same editorial integrity as the magazine that has brought you the most eclectic contemporary American poetry since 1969.

Books

nyqbooks.org

poetry at the edge™

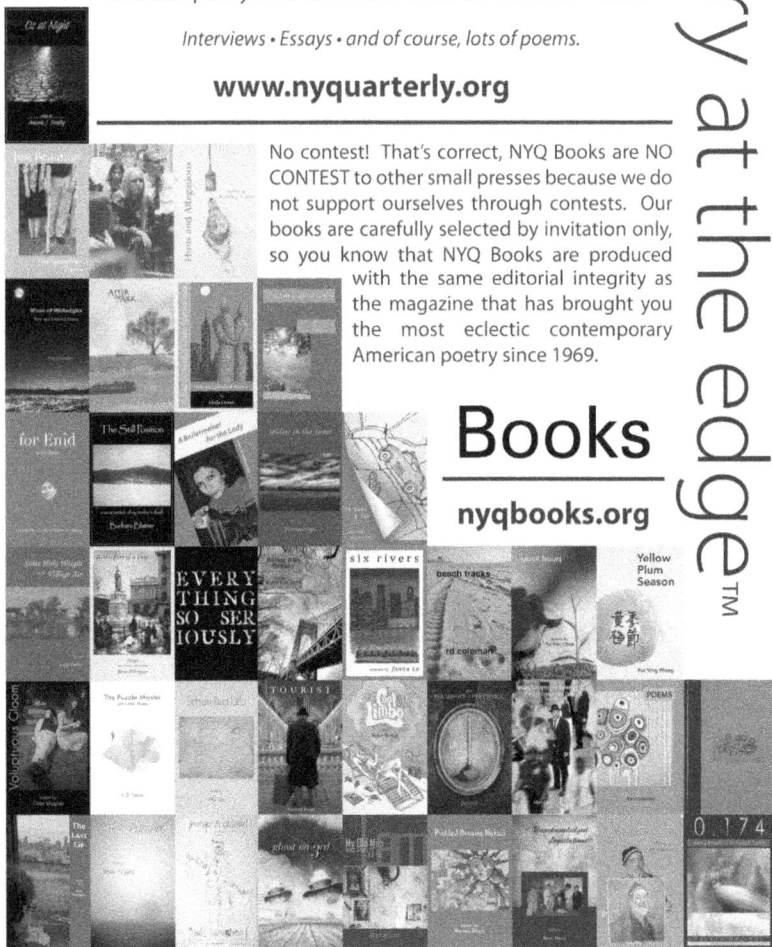

www.ingramcontent.com/pod-product-compliance
Lightning Source LLC
Chambersburg PA
CBHW022035090426
42741CB00007B/1068

9 781630 450434